First World War
and Army of Occupation
War Diary
France, Belgium and Germany

31 DIVISION
94 Infantry Brigade
Norfolk Regiment
12th Battalion
1 May 1918 - 24 May 1919

WO95/2366/2

The Naval & Military Press Ltd
www.nmarchive.com
Published in association with The National Archives

Published by

The Naval & Military Press Ltd

Unit 10 Ridgewood Industrial Park,

Uckfield, East Sussex,

TN22 5QE England

Tel: +44 (0) 1825 749494

www.naval-military-press.com

www.nmarchive.com

This diary has been reprinted in facsimile from the original. Any imperfections are inevitably reproduced and the quality may fall short of modern type and cartographic standards.

© **Crown Copyright**
Images reproduced by permission of The National Archives, London, England, 2015.

Contents

Document type	Place/Title	Date From	Date To
Heading	WO95/2366-2 12 Battalion Norfolk Regiment		
Heading	31st Division 94th Infy Bde 12th Bn Norfolk Regt May 1918 May 1919 From Egypt 74 Div 230 Bde		
Heading	74th Division 230th Infy Bde 31 Div 94 Bde 12th Bn Norfolk Regt May 1918 From Egypt		
War Diary	In The Field	01/05/1918	16/05/1918
War Diary	In The Field	07/05/1918	31/05/1918
Heading	War Diary Of The 12th Battalion Norfolk Regiment. June, 1918. May 19 Period: From June 1st, 1918. To June 30th 1918 Vol 4		
War Diary	B.E.F.	01/06/1918	30/06/1918
War Diary	B.E.F.	05/06/1918	30/06/1918
Heading	War Diary. 12th (Yeomanry) Battalion Norfolk Regiment. July 1918 Volume 2.		
War Diary	France	01/07/1918	31/07/1918
Heading	12th (Yeo) Battalion Norfolk Regiment War Diary for the month of August 1918 Volume III		
War Diary	In The Field	01/08/1918	16/08/1918
War Diary	Field	16/08/1918	31/08/1918
Heading	12th (Yeo) Bn. Norfolk Regt. War Diary from the 1st to 30th Sept. 1918 Vol 7		
War Diary	Field	01/09/1918	09/09/1918
War Diary	Field	08/09/1918	30/09/1918
Heading	War Diary of the 12th (Yeo.) Bn Norfolk Regt for the month of October 1918 Vol 11		
War Diary	France	01/10/1918	31/10/1918
War Diary	France	21/10/1918	21/10/1918
Heading	War Diary for November, 1918 12th (Yeo) Bn. R.S.F. Vol 12		
Heading	War Diary Of The 12th (Yeo) Bn Norfolk Rt. For November 1918 Vol 12		
War Diary	France	01/11/1918	30/11/1918
Heading	War Diary Of The 12th (Yeo.) Bn Norfolk. Regt. For Month Of December 1918 Vol 13		
War Diary	France	01/12/1918	20/12/1918
War Diary	France	14/12/1918	31/12/1918
War Diary		01/02/1919	28/02/1919
War Diary		01/03/1919	31/03/1919
War Diary	St Omer France	01/04/1919	30/04/1919
War Diary	St Omer France	01/05/1919	24/05/1919

WO/O5/2366

12

12 Battalion Norfolk Regiment.

31ST DIVISION
94TH INFY BDE

12TH ( ) BN NORFOLK REGT
MAY
~~JUNE~~ 1918 - MAY 1919

FROM EGYPT 74 DIV 230 BDE

Box 2366

ATTACHED { 74TH DIVISION
            230TH INFY BDE

31 DIV
94 Bde

12TH BN NORFOLK REGT

MAY 1918

FROM EGYPT

230/74

May/16
12 Norfolk Rgt

Army Form C. 2118.

WAR DIARY
or
INTELLIGENCE SUMMARY.

(Erase heading not required.)

Instructions regarding War Diaries and Intelligence Summaries are contained in F.S. Regs., Part II. and the Staff Manual respectively. Title pages will be prepared in manuscript.

Place	Date 1918	Hour	Summary of Events and Information	Remarks and references to Appendices
In the field	May 1 " 2nd to May 16		HMT Caledonia sailed at 3 p.m. from Gastari docks Alexandria. At Sea. At Ships inspection parade in the mornings. Gas drill and boat drill was carried out daily. Classes for instruction in Lewis Gun work for officers and N.C.O's were carried out daily under the Battn. Lewis Gun officer.	
	" 7		Arrived at Marseilles at 12 am. Battn disembarked at 2 pm. Rest of the baggage was stored at the docks under guard. The Battn marched to Rest camp at Musi Buron. Arriving there at 5 pm.	
	" 8		At Rest camp. A certain percentage of officers and men were allowed into Marseille during the afternoon/evening.	
	" 9		Battn left Rest camp at 5. am and marched to entraining point near the docks. Entrained at 7.30 am and left Marseille about 9 am.	
	10-11. 12		In train. Arrived at Noyelles sur Mer at 2 am. went into adjacent rest camp for remainder of the early hours. At 9 am Battn marched to Dannes Camp at Navarra arriving there about 11 am.	
	13-20		In camp at Navarra. On 16" lecture on bayonet fighting given to Battn. by Col. Campbell. Gas operations having carried out daily during this period. Reorganization of Battn made. New establishment was effected. 2/Lt. A.F. Moore rejoined Battn. from England.	
	21		Battn left in 2 parties, first party at 10 am second party at 12 pm. marched to entraining point at RUE Restaurant.	

Army Form C. 2118.

WAR DIARY
or
INTELLIGENCE SUMMARY.
(Erase heading not required.)

Place	Date	Hour	Summary of Events and Information	Remarks and references to Appendices
In the Field	May 22		Battn. arrived at LIGNY detrained and marched to MAISNIL-NEUVILLE-AU-CORNET where billets had been taken over by billeting party sent on in advance. 'D' Coy & Battn. HQ at MAISNIL, A B C Coys at NEUVILLE-AU-CORNET.	
	23-24		Training was continued	
	25		Battn. left at 9 a.m. marched to IZEL-LES-HAMEAU arriving there at 2 p.m. Took over billets, previously occupied by 116 Canadian Section.	
	26 to 31		Training continued. Special attention being paid to Gas drill, bayonet fighting at 200 yd range and 30 yd range rifle musketry practices carried out on and one. Musketry practices carried out under supervision of Bn. musketry officer.	

COURSES
========

2/Lieut G.R.K Jode & 4 n.c.o's attended a bayonet fighting course at Bell #8 whilst Battn. was at NOUVIONS.

Ct. Cracroft wanted "Good" at Rifle Grenade discharger course

Battn. classes held for instruction in special sight mounting of Lewis Guns.

W G Pickard
CAPT. & ADJT.
12TH. (YEO) BN. NORFOLK REGT.

CONFIDENTIAL.

WAR DIARY

OF

THE 12TH BATTALION NORFOLK REGIMENT.

JUNE, 1918.

PERIOD : From June 1st, 1918,
To June 30th, 1918.

WAR DIARY
or
INTELLIGENCE SUMMARY.
(Erase heading not required.)

Army Form C. 2118.

Place	Date	Hour	Summary of Events and Information	Remarks and references to Appendices
B.E.F.	1918. June 1st to 20th		The Batt continued to occupy Billets at IZEL LES HAMEAU, carrying on training normally 6 hours a day. Company Batt & Brigade Field Days were included in each weeks programme of work & proved very instructive to all ranks. Special demonstrations were arranged for the Division by the Tanks Corps, all Officers & a certain number of N.C.O's being detailed to attend these demonstrations. A certain period of each day was devoted to musketry training & all men fired a short course (25 rounds) on Rifle Ranges in the training area. The results proved quite satisfactory. When there was no Batt or Brigade Field Day all available time was devoted to the training of Specialists, Lewis Gunners, Signallers, Scouts & Bombers. The Divisional Gas Officer lectured the Batt on Gas & gave a Demonstration with Smoke Bombs & Lachrymatory Gas. Battalion Sports	
	16.			
	18.		The Batt witnessed an attack in conjunction with Tanks & in the afternoon 2 Coys practised similar attack with one section of Tanks.	
	20		News was received about 8 a.m. that the Batt was being transferred to the 31st Division as the Brigades of the 74th Divn had to be reduced to 3 Batt. At 12 noon the G.O.C. 74th Divn Major Gen. E.S. Girdwood C.B. visited the Batt & expressed his regret at having to part with this Batt. The day we arrived with the 31st Divn, the Commdg Officer received the following letter from Major Gen E. Girdwood.	

Army Form C. 2118.

WAR DIARY
or
INTELLIGENCE SUMMARY.
(Erase heading not required.)

Place	Date	Hour	Summary of Events and Information	Remarks and references to Appendices
	2/6/18		Dear Knox,
As you will understand I cannot issue a Special Order of the Day on your departure, at the same time I feel I cannot let you & your splendid men go without writing to tell you how sorry I am to lose you & them. The whole Yeomanry Division, & particularly myself, suffer an irreparable loss by the transfer of your gallant Battⁿ to another Division. No man has ever been better served than I have by the Norfolk Yeomanry or could wish to have under his Command a finer Battalion. Every objective that has been given them & all I have ever asked them to do they have done, & more than done, with never failing success & undaunted gallantry. Theirs is a record which few Battalions can equal & none surpass. We shall watch your deeds & follow your fortunes wherever you may be with intense interest & the feeling that although you are not with us, you are still of us, knowing the whole that whatever you are given to do will be carried through with that gallant yeoman spirit which knows not defeat & that devotion to duty which you have invariably displayed. On my own behalf & that of the whole Yeomanry Division I wish you & your gallant battalion God Speed & good fortune.

Yours sincerely
(signed) E. S. Girdwood Major General
Commanding 74th (Yeo) Division | |

Army Form C. 2118.

WAR DIARY
or
INTELLIGENCE SUMMARY.
(Erase heading not required.)

Place	Date	Hour	Summary of Events and Information	Remarks and references to Appendices
	June 21.		Entrained at TINQUES Station for BLARINGHAM. Arrived about 4.30 p.m. & were met by Brig. Genl. Comndg. 94th Inf. Bde., Genl. A. Symons, C.M.G. Were billeted at BLARINGHAM	
	22/3.		Battn. re-organised, & also passed through Gas Test	
	24th		Battn. marched to D.20. t.9.6. (Ref. Sheet 36a. N.E.) & remained one night	
	25th		At night took over the line from 10th E. Yorks Regt. A. Coy. but Sect. Coy. neighbourhood of E.28.c.R.4.a. B. & D. Coys. in supports in E.27. c.r.d. & K.3.a. C. Coy. in Reserve in E.27.a. Battn. H.Q. at FETTLE FARM. D 24 a. 8.2	
	27/28.		Battn. was relieved at night by 12th R.S.F. & marched to positions as follows:— coming under orders of the 93rd Infantry Bde. A. Coy. to SWARTENBROUCK. E.14. t. D. " to PETIT SEC BOIS E.9.C. B. & C. Coys to GRANDE MARQUETTE FARM E.7.a. Battn. H.Q. at D.6, d.9.8	
	26.		The 31st Divn. attacked at 6 a.m. taking all objectives.	
	29.		The Battn. was not called upon during the day & remained in above positions. B. Coy. found Carrying Party of 1.90 other ranks. Orders were received at 1.20 a.m. to move back to D.20. t.9.6. where all Coys. joined the Battn. which again came under orders of the 94th Inf. Bde.	
	30.		On the night of June 30th/July 1st the 94th Bde. took over the line with the 12th R.S.F. on the Right, 24th R.W.F. on the left, 12th Norfolks in Reserve.	

WAR DIARY
or
INTELLIGENCE SUMMARY.
(Erase heading not required.)

Army Form C. 2118.

The Battalion was disposed as under:-

Coy in old support line
C & B. Coys in line in wood just west of "A. RIDE" E.27.b.&.d
A & D " in Brigade Reserve in E.25.d.
Battn H.Q. at E.25.a.7.9

Health. With the exception of an epidemic of Influenza which broke out in the Regiment about the middle of the month & reduced our strength by 200 in one week, the health of the troops has been good.

Casualties between June 24th & 30th were 1 Officer wounded, 1 O.R. killed 5 O.R. wounded.

Effective Strength June 30th. 36 Officers 780 O.R.

W G Riddell
Captain & Adjt.
for O.C. 12th (4to) Batt. Norfolk Regiment.

CONFIDENTIAL.

WAR DIARY.

12TH (YEOMANRY) BATTALION NORFOLK REGIMENT.

JULY 1918

VOLUME 2.

PERIOD : From July 1st, 1918.
To July 31st, 1918.

Army Form C. 2118.

WAR DIARY
or
INTELLIGENCE SUMMARY.
(Erase heading not required.)

Place	Date	Hour	Summary of Events and Information	Remarks and references to Appendices
France	1/7/18		Ref. Map. Sheet 36 A.N.E. 1/20.000. On the night of the 30th June/1st July the 94th Infantry Brigade relieved the 92nd Infantry Brigade in the right sector of the Divisional Front. This unit went in Brigade Reserve. Batt. H.Q. was situated at E.25.b.6.9. B. & C. Coys occupied breastworks in E.27.b.+d. A. & D. Coys in Reserve line in E.19.c	
	2/7/18		A & D Coys moved across the road to E.25.b. still being in the reserve line.	
	3/7/18		On the night of July 3rd/4th the Battn relieved the 12th R.S.F. in the right sector of the Brigade Front. A & D Coys in front line posts. K.5.d.51 – LE CORNET PERDU K 5 d 95 – K 6 a 30 – GARS BRUGGHE K.5.d.98. B & C Coys occupied the main line of resistance from K.4.c.53 to E.28.c.62 "B" on the right, "C" on the left. Batt. H.Q. at E.27.d.7.7 Note Lt. Col Moose acts. a Capt Harbord J. wounded	
	5/7/18		Inter Company relief. "B" Coy relieving "A" Coy & "C" Coy relieving "D" Coy	
	7/7/18			
	8/7/18		On the night of July 8th/9th one platoon of A Coy & one platoon of D Coy carried out a small enterprise assisted by a detachment of 211th Field Coy R.E with the object of blowing up two bridges over the BECQUE one at K 11 & 44 & one at K 12 a 34	

WAR DIARY
or
INTELLIGENCE SUMMARY
(Erase heading not required.)

Army Form C. 2118.

Place	Date	Hour	Summary of Events and Information	Remarks and references to Appendices
France	8/7/18 Contd.		2/Lt. H. Wagner with D Coy Platoon attained his object & succeeded in blowing up bridge at K.11.b.94. 2/Lt. J.C. Knox with A Coy platoon came up against superior opposition from enemy M.G. in farm at K.12.a.2.7 and a post occupied by the enemy about K.6.c.3.0.6. This prevented him from getting near bridge which was his objective. K.6.c.6.2.	
	9/7/18		On the following night 2/Lt J.C. Knox went out again with his platoon with the object of occupying the farm at K.12.a.2.7 & if possible blowing up bridge at K.12.a.34. He succeeded in occupying the farm & establishing a post of 1 NCO & 6 men there. He reconnoitred forward himself but on approaching the bridge found it swept by enemy M.G. fire from the front & both flanks. He decided that without Artillery bombardment it was not practicable to blow up the bridge.	
	10-11/7/18		On the night of 10/11th July the Brigade was relieved on the line by the 96th Infantry Brigade, this unit being relieved by the 18th Durham L.I. On relief the Battalion marched back to D.19.a.7.8 & the Brigade came into Divisional Reserve for six days.	
	13/7/18		Battalion Transport was inspected by B.G.C. 94th Brigade.	
	13/7/18		The Batt'n. was inspected by B.G.C. 94th Bde. & afterwards marched past in fours.	
	14/7/18		Inspection of the 94th Inf. Bde. by Lieut. General Sir Beauvoir de Lisle commanding XV Army Corps. This was followed by a Church Parade service to which the Corps Commander remained. He expressed himself very pleased with the bearing & turnout of the men.	

Army Form C. 2118.

WAR DIARY
or
INTELLIGENCE SUMMARY.
(Erase heading not required.)

Instructions regarding War Diaries and Intelligence Summaries are contained in F. S. Regs., Part II. and the Staff Manual respectively. Title pages will be prepared in manuscript.

Place	Date	Hour	Summary of Events and Information	Remarks and references to Appendices
France	16/7/18		On the night of the 16/17th July the Brigade again moved up into the line to relieve 92nd Inf. Bde., this time in the left Sector of Divisional Front. The battalion went into Reserve relieving the 11th E. Yorks Regt. Disposition of Companies: "D" Coy in Main Line of Resistance at PETIT SEC BOIS about E.9.d.16. "A" Coy in Reserve Line E.13.d. "C" Coy in "B" line defence at GRAND MARQUETTE FARM — E.7.a. "B" Coy at LA PROMENADE — D.12.a.31. Batt. HQ at D.6.a.96.	
17/7/18		The XV Corps Cyclist Batt⁵ went up to strengthen the right sector of the Brigade Front & who relieved our Batt⁵ from the neighbourhood of one Company holding the Reserve Line in E.13.d., Consequently "A" Coy moved back to "B" line defences in E.7.a. & on the right of "C" Coy.	
17/20th July		Working parties were found each night for work under the Divl Pioneer Battn. (12th KOYLI) in improving & strengthening the Main Line of Resistance about E.15.a+c.	
20/7/18		On the night of 20/21st July the Battn moved up into the front line taking over the right sector of the Brigade Front from the 12th R.S.F. The two companies of XV Corps Cyclist Bn came under Command of this unit. The line extended from E.29.b.2.5. to E.17.c.6.5. was then held by one Coy of Cyclist Batt⁵ on the right with one platoon of "B" Coy in close support & "A" Coy on the left.	

WAR DIARY
or
INTELLIGENCE SUMMARY.

Army Form C. 2118.

Place	Date	Hour	Summary of Events and Information	Remarks and references to Appendices
France	20/7/18 contd.		"C" Coy went into the Main Line of Resistance in E.15.d. "B" Coy (less one platoon) & "D" Coy occupied the Reserve Line running from E.13.d.1.3. to E.14.b.4.10. "B" Coy on the right & "D" Coy on the left. Battn. H.Q. at SWARTENBROUCK — E.14.b.5.3.	
	22/7/18		It was decided to further strengthen the front line, to do this "B" Coy went up to the outpost line on the left of "A" Coy, took over the right hand post of the Batts on our left & the left hand post of "A" Coy. At the same time "A" Coy took over the left post held by the Cyclist Coy. This meant that the outpost line was then held by one Coy of the Cyclist Batt's in the right Sub Sector with one platoon in the line & one in support; "A" Coy in the centre sub sector with three platoons in the line & one in support; "B" Coy in the left sub sector with two platoons in the front line & two in support. "C" Coy remained in its original position in Main Line of Resistance & "D" Coy in Reserve Line. Patrols were sent out both by day & night from the Outpost Companies & very useful information was gained by them.	
	24/7/18		On the night of July 24/25th, inter Company Reliefs took place "A" Coy being relieved by "C" Coy & "B" Coy being relieved by "D" Coy	

WAR DIARY
or
INTELLIGENCE SUMMARY.

Army Form C. 2118.

Place	Date	Hour	Summary of Events and Information	Remarks and references to Appendices
France	26th/27th 7/18		On the night 26th/27th July two platoons of "A" Coy under Major H.Q. Birkbeck carried out a raid on enemy posts on the east side of the Becque. The left group Artillery & the 31st Machine Gun Batt. co-operated in this raid. The raiding party when the Artillery Barrage lifted rushed the enemy posts, but were only in time to see the enemy numbering about 20, running away. Casualties 5 wounded, 2 missing.	
	28/7/18		On the night of the 28th/29th the 94th Infantry Brigade was relieved by the 93rd Infantry Brigade, this unit being relieved by the 13th York & Lancaster Regt.	
	29/7/18		After relief the Battn marched back to Rest Camp D.19.a.6.7. the 94th Brigade coming into Divisional Reserve.	
	30th & 31st 7/18		Company Training. Effective Strength 40 Officers 956 Other Ranks.	

W.E. Russell
Capt & adjt.

for 12th Commanding Officer

12th BATTALION.
NORFOLK REGIMENT.

94/31   No 6

12th (Yeo) Battalion Norfolk Regiment

War Diary

for the month of August 1918.

Volume III

WAR DIARY
or
INTELLIGENCE SUMMARY

Army Form C. 2118.

Place	Date	Hour	Summary of Events and Information	Remarks and references to Appendices
In the Field	1/8/18			
	2/8/18	15	The Battalion completed its period of rest and reserve at D.19.a. (Sheet 36 A/1/20000) near MORBECQUE	
	3/8/18		The Battalion relieved the Durham Light Infantry in the line at SWARTEN BROUCK about 11 pm. with two Companies (A+B) C-D Companies were left behind to proceed to new rest camp area at L.30.a.9.7 near WALLON CAPPELLE there to meet tents and prepare for the reception of the remainder of the Bn. The second in Command and Major H.E. Barclay commanded the two companies in the line.	MAP REF. Sheet 36 A NE 1/20000
	4th		At about 12 midnight the two companies were relieved by the 23rd Lancs. Fusiliers. The Fusiliers took over also part of the line on our right held by the Cyclist Bn. On relief our two companies under Major H.E. Barclay marched to the new rest camp area at L.30.a.9.7 arriving there about 6. a.m. A the 5th.	
	5th-10th		This period was spent in reorganizing the Bn. Coy & battalion training, specialist training and recreation. During this period the Bn. lines the wood near WALLON CAPPELLE behind HTH. Thinking drove past in his car. A party also was sent to represent the Bn. in a Corps parade which was subsequently inspected by H.M. The King on Aug 10th	
	11th		The Battalion moved out of the rest camp about 6.30 pm and marched by easy stages to relieve the 12" R.S.F. in support at GRANDE MARQUETTE. The relief was completed about 11.50 pm. A+B coy at the farm E.7.a.3.9. C. Cy at D.6.a.5.4. D Coy at E.8.d.5.7. BN. H.Q. at E.I.C.O.8.	
	12th - 14th		The Battalion remained in support on the same disposition with the exception of A+C Coys who were moved to SANITA'S CORNER to be nearer the line which was gradually being advanced	
	15th		The Battalion relieved the 12 RSF in the line, C+D Coy in the line, B Coy in support, A Coy in 2nd line remaining at SANITA'S CORNER. Relief was completed about midnight	
	16th		Our platoon of D Coy under 2nd Lt. E.P. Smith was detailed to raid enemy strong points in E.18.d.05.60 and E.18.d.05.70 with the concurrence of the Artillery. At Zero hour which was fixed at 2:30 pm the raiding party started. At 3 pm some rifle fire and M.G. fire was opened. As this fire continued as per instructions received from Brigade, artillery support was called for, which dropped a barrage on supposed enemy supports behind the strong points. Enfr. diagram attached nothing was seen of the raiding party for sometime and M.G. rifle fire continued in short bursts. The Left a/c under Sgt Maude, after advancing 150-200 yds approx came upon a line of 3 POSTS containing 10-12 men each.	Do

WAR DIARY
or
INTELLIGENCE SUMMARY
(Erase heading not required.)

Army Form C. 2118.

(2)

Place	Date	Hour	Summary of Events and Information	Remarks and references to Appendices
Field	16/8/18		This left section consisted of 14 men & the noncom minutes the section was forced to withdraw owing to enemy quickly working round their right flank and the right section. This enemy Posts are reputed by Sgt Walden to be about 30-50 yds in front of the N clump of trees. In between these posts the line there appears to be some men in course of section movements. The left section withdraws 20 yds down a minor ditch repaired fire in the enemy. Seeing that 2/Lt Smith who was in charge of the raiding party who was killed during the action did not see the enemy working in between the two sections Sgt Walden and Cpl Lent sent man runners down across to warn him but these two men could not get there in time to be of any use as at that moment the enemy started to bomb the right section. Shortly after the right section began to gradually withdraw. The left section then opened fire to cover the withdrawal of the right section & gradually withdrew another 50 yds when they again opened fire to cover right action withdrawal. Having given Sgt. Wright action to get tract the operation then withdraws to the original outpost line Sgt right design. From various accounts of NCO & men in his section it appears that the second in front of small clumps of trees was manned by an enemy garrison of from 40-60 men. This section was given the orders to charge & by 2/Lt Smith ran meeting the stand. They were heavily bombed causing many casualties. 2/Lt Smith & perhaps runners man got into a section of the enemy trench. It then appears that 2/Lt Smith seeing that he cannot get on gave the order to withdraw. 2/Lt R. Heading who was in charge of the supporting platoon seeing that the raiding party was withdrawing & appeared to be in difficulties immediately pushed forward his platoon so as to cover its retirement of the right section. Failing up & pushing he opened fire on the enemy rifle light section withdrew in an orderly manner. Though his platoon 2/Lt Heading then gradually withdrew also. A M.G. marked ⓧ in which appear to have worked round to the right flank of the right section which was engaged by our right Lewis Gun which was killed the M gun which was already damaged was unfortunately lost. One Lewis Gun section of the left Company that was pushed forward to Corn the flank of the raiding party carried out the following movements in conjunction. They crawled up to a ditch at E.19.d.05.07 where there was a small enemy listening post which ran away when he ditch. They took up a position covering the flank. When the raiding party attacked they observed right of the enemy run away and twelve fired forward to what they took to be a small post. They fired several magazines and at least 10 casualties were observed to be inflicted	

WAR DIARY
or
INTELLIGENCE SUMMARY.
(Erase heading not required.)

Army Form C. 2118.

Place	Date	Hour	Summary of Events and Information	Remarks and references to Appendices
Field	16/5/16		When the raiding party had withdrawn they support back to the Lydt line. Sgt Zennard who went out to form liaison between the raiding party & right platoon of left Company arrived when enemy standing. Thereupon he let two off him. Sgt going into action 1 Off + 30 o.r. Casualties 1 Off killed, 11 or wounded	
	17/5/16		Relief were carried out. B Coy relieved C Coy in the line & D platoon of D. remained of Bn. then going in close support. Patrols were sent out ascertain amount of wiring done.	Map ref. Sheet 36A. NE 1/20000.
	18/5/16		In conjunction with the 9th Bde situation Operations were projected for obtaining the fighting patrols were detailed to make patrol whose main work to capture the strong point at E.18.d.05.70 Our patrols had orders not to move unless it was seen that the Bn on left had taken their first objective. Our patrols toon up their battle positions, but it appears that the Bn on our left, running up against superior resistance were forced to withdraw and therefore that our patrols lay in their battle positions most of the day who withdrew at night without having accomplished any of the objectives they went to attain.	
	19/5/16		In conjunction with the 8th Bde an an all the Bn was detailed to attack enemy positions being from a given to final objective F.13.c.9.9 to LABIS FARM hence following the VIEUX BERQUIN WAY to COURRIE COTTAGE. The artillery programme was as follows: Barrage to start at ZERO hour and continue (with a width of 6 minutes lift by horngs) with following A/R-100yds every 3 minutes until reaching final objective, then to rest 250yds, in front of them. Enemy returns attack anything MG's concentrated at B+C Coy work's action, and C Coy + RSF borrowing - two from D Coy were to consolidate the new line being an enemy position E.18.d.05.75. The Bn. formed up in its assembly posns. which was 50 yds behind the line of its emergency to the line, by 4 p.m. LERO having proof barrage opened the line we'd forward, keeping well up with the enemy immediately as shown. The enemy being traced by the enemy than nearing the 1st and first captured by the enemy causing many casualties among the	Map ref. LABIS. FM. 1/10000

WAR DIARY or INTELLIGENCE SUMMARY

Army Form C. 2118.

Place	Date	Hour	Summary of Events and Information	Remarks and references to Appendices
Field	19/8/18		Thus causing the right flank to be held up, also the left was held up by machine gun snipers. The two left platoons (A Coy) had closed until too much to the left, thus leaving some of the enemy strong point at E.18.d.05.70 untouched. O.C. D Coy seeing this immediately pushed forward his right hand platoon engaging the enemy. A Then brought up the remainder of D Coy forming a line with A Coy right, pushed forward, taking every strong point at E.18.a.9.8 taking prisoners at E.18.d.1.1. The enemy fell back fighting all the way to about where a series party of B Coy then pushed forward to within a short distance of the final objective, overcoming considerable resistance on the part of enemy counter snipers who were concealed in shell holes. This party seeing that the flanks were held up and took up reinforcement. There came up causing the enemy to relieve themselves, the flank 15 more forward to final objective, overcoming & very considerable resistance from numerous hostile snipers concealed in Recom. The whole line was in final objective, causing many casualties to retreating enemy. The right hand guard went then considerable and destroying huts were immediately pushed forward. A cleaning party which was formed by D Coy and part gained. The enemy put down a heavy barrage in front of our new line, but apparently were not aware at it had established our line. Prisoners Taken 60. M.G's captured 12. Casualties. Killed - 8 officers. 38 o.r. Wounded 1 offr. 100 o.r. O.r. 100 enemy decad apart counted on the field. Our line was further consolidated and patrols pushed forward to locate enemy.	Map ref Sheet 36 a N E 1/20,000
	20/8/18			
	21/8/18		Relieved early in the morning on the line by the 2nd R.W.S. Bn moved back to support, 1 Coy in TERN FARM line at VIEUX BERQUIN and 3 Coy on Z line trenches at SANITA'S CORNER.	
	22/8/18		The Bn was relieved about 6 p.m. by the 12 Nork. Staff Regt. and marched back by Coy to our Camp area at D.19.a.6.7 near MORBECQUE arriving there about 11.30 p.m.	
	23/8/18		The Battalion was relieved at D.19.a.6.7 about 6 p.m. by the Royal Irish (40 Bn) and marched together with our transport to bus section arriving about 9.30 p.m. at V.10.a.8.2. Transport lines at V.11.	Map ref Sheet 27 1/40,000

Army Form C. 2118.

WAR DIARY
or
INTELLIGENCE SUMMARY.
(Erase heading not required.)

(5)

Place	Date	Hour	Summary of Events and Information	Remarks and references to Appendices
Zeel.	24/8/18		The Battalion was relieved by the 11' Essex about 5 pm and moving out at 8 pm marched to X.1.6.95.15. relieving the Black Watch in support in this area, with Bn. H.Q at X.1.6.95.15. The route taken to this area was via CAESTRE & FLETRE.	Map ref Sheet 27 1/40000
	25th to 26.		In support.	
	27/8/18.		The Battalion relieved the 12' Royal Scots in the line in X 7's square about midnight. C & D Coys on the line, A & B in close support, Bn H.Q. at X.5.a.5.3. (KOPJE FARM).	B°
	28th 29th		On alert in the line. Line was patrolled nightly. On the night of the 29 one (1) my patrols encountered an enemy post. Our casualties were 1 offcr wounded missing 1 O.R. killed 2 O.R. missing.	
	30th		During the morning the enemy was reported to have evacuated his position. Patrols were immediately pushed out & it was reported that the enemy had retired to a ridge 800 to 1000 yds beyond BAILLEUL. The Brigade on our flank then pushed forward thereby obtaining our line, thus compelling our brigade to conform from the line. The Battalion then about 9.30 pm marched to X.1.6.31. where it was placed with the remainder of the Brigade in Divisional reserve.	
	31st		Battalion in same area.	

WAR DIARY
or
INTELLIGENCE SUMMARY.

(Erase heading not required.)

Army Form C. 2118.

Place	Date	Hour	Summary of Events and Information	Remarks and references to Appendices
Hill			At the conclusion of the Aug 19" Operation the following messages were received by the Battalion:— To Genl. DE LISLE. Early 15 Corps please accept my congratulations and convey them again to the Commanders of the 29, 31, 35 Divisions and all troops engaged yesterday on Kiway Key planned & carried out & having very successful operation yesterday afternoon. From Genl. PLUMER. From Corps Commander. — "Corps Commander notes & pleased with the success of your minor operation and wishes you to convey his appreciation to the troops concerned." "Please express to all ranks the Divisional Commander's appreciation of the most excellent work done by all Officers, N.C.O.s & men during the minor operation yesterday. Success was largely due to the skilful planning of the operation and the excellent cooperation between Artillery & Infantry. Plans hence, and the men displayed the fine fighting spirit which enabled the 12 (Yks) Bn Norfolk Regt. to overcome strong opposition. (Sgd) M H Annesley H Col. A.A/D.M.G. 31 Div. During the month the following courses were attended by H.M.S Battalion at various courses. Lewis Gun Courses G.H.Q. Course. Cpl. Repps — Grade 2 H/C Anglin — Good. H/C Kirby — V. Good. XV Corps Course. Pte P.T. Course Mj Knox — V. Good Sgt Rix — V. Good. Cpl Morfitt — Good. H/C Arlott — Good "Hanies — Good. Musketry 1st Army Course 2/L Smith — distinguished Sgt Edwards — very good " Wilson — Good " Brick — Fair XV Corps Gas Course H/C Orsenf — Per gas N.C.o. H/C Webb — Do H/C Greaves — Cpl Sr	

Army Form C. 2118.

WAR DIARY
or
INTELLIGENCE SUMMARY.
(Erase heading not required.)

Place	Date	Hour	Summary of Events and Information	Remarks and references to Appendices
Field	31/8/18		Effective Strength R.	
			29 Officers	
			986 ORs.	

In the field.
Sep. 2 1918.

J. H. Stanley, Major.
Commanding 12 (Yeo) Bn. Norfolk Regt.

12th (Sev.) Bn. Norfolk Regt.

War Diary

from the 1st to 30th Sep. 1918

Army Form C. 2118.

WAR DIARY
or
INTELLIGENCE SUMMARY.
(Erase heading not required.)

Place	Date	Hour	Summary of Events and Information	Remarks and references to Appendices
Field	4/9/16 5/9/16		The Battalion remained at FAUNA FARM X.l.b.3.l. until Sept.4th. when the brigade moved forward to BAILLEUL.	
			The night 4/5th. was spent at BAILLEUL & on the 5th. the brigade moved forward & relieved the 86th. & 88th.brigades of the 29th. Division.	
			The line was taken overby the 12th. R.i.S.F. &24th. R.W.F., this battalion being in support with Battalion Headquarters at T.28.a.4.2.	
			Disposition of Companies	
			"A" Coy. at T.11.d. "B" Coy. at T.17.a. being lent to 24th.R.W.F. as support.	
			"C" & "D" Coys. in the G.H.Q. line from T.22.a. _ T.28.a.	
			Remained in support in the above positions.	
	6/9/16		On the night of the 8/9th. the battalion relieved the 12th.R.S.F. in the right sector from HYDE PARK CORNER U.19..b.4.8. inclusive U.19.c.7.1.	
	20/9/16		U.25.d.0.0. _ C.l.b.2.0.	
			B Coy. on the left from U.19.b.4.8. U.19.c.7.1.	
			D Coy. on the right from U.19.c.7.1. _ U.25.d.0.0.	
			1 platoon of C.Coy. on D Coy's. right from U.25.d.0.0. _ C.l.b.2.0.	
			Remaining platoons of C.Coy. were in support about T.30.c.8d.	
			A Coy. in support at T.23.d.8.8.	
			Battalion Headquarters at PETITE MUNQUE FARM at T.23.d.8.8.	
			From the 8th. to the 13th. the battalion held this position on the battalion front. Patrols were pushed out in daylight & each night & much useful information about the enemy was obtained.	
	8/13 9/16		On the night of Sept.13th./14th.the battalion was relieved by the 15th WEST YORK Regiment.93rd.Brigade & marched back to bivouac area at S.14.d.9.8. The Brigade was then in support to the 93rd. Brigade who held the line.	
	13/14 9/16		The Battalion spent 5 days in this camp which was devoted to re-organising & company training.	
	14/19 9/16		On the night of 18/19th.Sept. the brigade took over the line from the 93rd. Brigade, this unit relieving the 18th.D.L.I. in support.	
	18/19 9/16		A Coy. was attached to the 12th. R.S.F. on the Right and B Coy. to the 24th. R.W.F. on the Left, both Companies occupying positions in the NIEPPE SYSTEM.	
			"C" Coy. in support at T.19.a.9.5.	
			"D" Coy. in support at T.25.b.1.8.	
			Bn.H.Q. at Aldershot Camp T.19.d.9.9.	

Army Form C. 2118.

WAR DIARY
or
INTELLIGENCE SUMMARY.
(Erase heading not required).

Instructions regarding War Diaries and Intelligence Summaries are contained in F. S. Regs., Part II. and the Staff Manual respectively. Title pages will be prepared in manuscript.

Place	Date	Hour	Summary of Events and Information	Remarks and references to Appendices
Field	9/9/18		The Battalion remained in above positions whilst the Brigade was in the line. Working parties were found by "C" & "D" Coys. both by day & night under Brigade arrangements.	Ref. Ploegsteert 1/10,000.
	23/9/18		Lt. Col. J. SHERWOOD KELLY V.C.C.M.G. D.S.O. took over command of the Battalion from MAJOR M.F. BARCLAY, who had been acting in place of Lt. Col. J.F. BARCLAY whilst the on leave.	
	24/9/18		The Battalion was relieved by the 11th. EAST LANCS REGIMENT 92nd. Brigade & marched back to BAILLEUL, where we entrained for HAZEBROUCK, arriving there about 2a.m. The Battalion moved into billets alloted to them. The Brigade was then in divisional Reserve and expected to be there for 12 days training. The first two days were devoted to cleaning up, refitting, and Training under Company Arrangements.	
	27/9/18		Owing to forthcoming operations the Brigade was moved up again to BAILLEUL in support. The Battalion entrained at HAZEBROUCK at 9a.m. arriving at BAILLEUL at 9.45a.m. & marched to bivouac area at A.9.4.5.3. Here we remained the day, at night orders were received to move on to camp vacated by 15th. WEST YORKS at T.26.c.4.3. The Battalion moved at 10.35p.m. & on arrival at T.26.c.4.3. at about 1.a.m. further orders were received to push on through NEUVE EGLISE to BAKERY POST at U.14.a.	
	28/9/18		The Battalion arrived there at dawn & went forward in Artillery Formation in support to the 93rd. Brigade with whomtouch was soon gained. "B" Coy. worked along the right of the road, & "A" Coy. along left of road. "D" Coy. moved out about 200 yards in rear & in support to "B" Coy. & "C" Coy. at a similar distance behind "A" Coy. After touch was obtained with the 93rd. Brigade the dispositions of the Coys was as under, "A" Coy. at U.9.c.7.8. "B" Coy. at U.15.c.2.5. "C" Coy. at U.9.c.5.3. "D" Coy. at U.15.c.1.0. The Battalion remained here until dusk, when the Battalion concentrated about ST. IVES TRENCH U.15.D- "B" & "A" Coys. formed up in trenches ULTIMO AVENUE at U.16. central "B" Coy. on the left & "A" Coy. on the right.	

Army Form C. 2118.

WAR DIARY
or
INTELLIGENCE SUMMARY.
(Erase heading not required.)

Instructions regarding War Diaries and Intelligence Summaries are contained in F. S. Regs., Part II. and the Staff Manual respectively. Title pages will be prepared in manuscript.

Place	Date	Hour	Summary of Events and Information	Remarks and references to Appendices
Field	30/9/18		"C" & "D" Coys. took up position about ST. IVES TRENCH. The Battalion attacked at dawn 4 a.m. FIRST OBJECTIVE; DUCKBOARD TRACK right resting at U 16.c.5.0. & left resting at U.17.c.2.8. This first objective was taken by "A" & "B" Coys. before dawn without opposition. "C" & "D" Coys. moved out of assembly trenches ULTIMO AVENUE when the first objective was taken, went through "A" & "B" Coys and took the SECOND OBJECTIVE. PLOEGSTEERT — WARNETON ROAD. Right resting at. U.22.c.9.8. and left resting WEST OF TROIS TILLEULS at U.17.c.6.4. without opposition.	
		At 5p.m.	orders were received to withdraw the two rear coys. ("A" & "B") leaving "C" & "D" under Capt. Ruggles Brise to be withdrawn when he was satisfied that the 92nd & 93rd. Brigades were in touch and were covering his front. On completion of withdrawal. Coys marched back independently to old bivouac area.at.A.9.a.5.3. The last Coy. marching in at 2.30 a.m. Total casualties during phase of operations 2 officers & 3 other ranks killed 15 other ranks wounded. During the month the following resul 's were obtained by the Battalion at various courses	

15 h CORPS N.C.O's. COURSE   MUSKETRY COURSE HAYLING ISLAND
320028 Sgt. Adcock T. GOOD   320015 Sgt. Thorpe L. GOOD
320116 Sgt Walker W. EXELENT.
320213 Sgt Newby W. V.GOOD

15th. CORPS GAS SCHOOL   15th. CORPS BOMBING SCHOOL
320183 L/c. Cooke A.   320745 L/c. Henderson J. GOOD
The following decorations were awarded to members of the Battalion
for gallantry during the action of VIEUX BERQUIN on August 19th.
Lt. L.W.P.Richards M.C. 320520 Sgt. R.T.Hase D.C.M.
30.558 Sgt. W.E.Snowling M.M. 320519 Cpl. A.R.Bunning M.M.
320629 Pte. A. Watts M.M. 320264 Sgt. J.H.Gunton M.M.
320877 Cpl. W.C.Lloyd M.M.   26458 Cpl. J.Lawn M.M.
320726 Pte. W.Gladwin M.M.
EFFECTIVE STRENGTH 30/9/18   OFFICERS 36   OTHER RANKS 784.

[signature]
Lt. Col.
Commanding 12th. (YEO.) BATTALION
NORFOLK REGIMENT

Vol 11

War Diary
of the

12th (Yeo.) Bn Norfolk Regt.

for the Month of October 1918

WAR DIARY
or
INTELLIGENCE SUMMARY.
(Erase heading not required.)

Army Form C. 2118.

Instructions regarding War Diaries and Intelligence Summaries are contained in F.S. Regs., Part II. and the Staff Manual respectively. Title pages will be prepared in manuscript.

Place	Date	Hour	Summary of Events and Information	Remarks and references to Appendices
France	1918 Oct 1/5		The Battalion remained in Bivouac Area at A.9.a.5.3. General Training was carried out.	
	Oct 6/7		On the night of the 6/7th. the Battalion relieved the 15th. West York Regt. in the line in the PLOEGSTEERT Sector with Bn. H.Q.at U.27.b.9.2 C.&D.Coys went in the line on the right & left respectively with A. & B. Coys. in right & left Support. As the march was a lengthy one, the Battalion staged at LE ROMARIN(B.4.a.) where a hot meal was provided. The line was held in the above manner. Continuous patrolling of the river LYS was maintained during the period.	
	Oct 7/8		On the night of the 8th. the following inter Company reliefs took place:- A Coy. relieved D Coy. in the line. B Coy. relieved C Coy. in the line. The line was held in the above manner and patrol activity was maintained On the morning of the 11th. two feint attacks were carried out with. the idea of the enemy thinking an attack was to take place. These feints took the form of an Artillery Creeping Barrage opening for 10 mins. on the enemy front line trenches and lifting every four minutes for about four lifts and continuing as a box Barrage for a further 10 mins. to give the enemy the impression that an attempt was about to be made to cross the LYS. The first Objective was C.5.Central to U.29.d.95.95. with Zero hour at 0545. The second Objective was U.24.a.2.5. to U.18.central with zero hour at 1015. Heavy Artillery cooperated by bombarding EPPELINGHEIM and U.30.c. in the first instance and DRULEMONT and V.b.c. and to do counter Battery work in the second instance. Smoke was used in the first but not in the second feint.	
	Oct 11		A Patrol from A Coy. was sent out early in the morning with the intention of attempting to cross the LYS by a bridge, but was stopped by machine gun fire. Very small enemy retaliatory fire was encountered as a result of these feint attacks. Lieut Col. J. SHERWOOD KELLY V.C. C.M.G. D.S.O. assumed command of the 94th. (Yeo) Infantry Brigade in the absence of Brig. Gen. Symons.C.M.G. on leave. Major H.A.Birkbeck M.M. assumed command of 12th. (Yeo) Battln. Norfolk Regiment. During this period in the line 10 rounds rapid was fired daily by each man.	

WAR DIARY
or
INTELLIGENCE SUMMARY.
(Erase heading not required.)

Army Form C. 2118.

Instructions regarding War Diaries and Intelligence Summaries are contained in F.S. Regs., Part II. and the Staff Manual respectively. Title pages will be prepared in manuscript.

Place	Date 1918	Hour	Summary of Events and Information	Remarks and references to Appendices
France	Oct 12th		On the night of the 12/13th. the Battalion was relieved in the line by the 11th. Battln. E.Lancs. On completion of relief the Battalion marched back by Coys. to Billets at BAILLEUL.	
	Oct 13/15		This period was spent in Billets at BAILLEUL refitting,reorganizing and training.	
	Oct 16th		The Battalion relieved the 13th D.L.I. in support at T.19.d.8.9.	
	Oct 17th		The Battalion moved to vicinity of PLOEGSTEERT occupying dugouts in old German trench system.	
	Oct 18th		The Battalion moved to QUESNOY, crossing the LYS via WARNETON occupying billets in the town. The same day about 2100 the Battalion moved to LE CHIEN occupying billets in the village.	
	Oct 19th		Lieut.Col.J.SHERWOOD KELLY V.C. C.M.G. D.S.O. reassumed command of 12th.(Yeo). Battln Norfolk Regt.on return of Brig. Gen Symons C.M.G. from leave	
	Oct 20	At 0800	the Battalion moved out and marched to LANNOY (L.10.c.c.) and occupied billets in the town. Training was carried out during this period and men were inoculated	
	Oct 21/24 Oct 25	At 1045	the Battalion moved out and marched to MOUSCRON and occupied billets. Men who were inoculated and other lorries.	
	Oct 26th		The Battalion moved out of MOUSCRON at 0930 and marched to STACEGHEM and occupied billets.	
	Oct 27th		The Battalion moved out of STACEGHEM at 1330 and marched to huts in I.20.b.central. where it came into support to the 92nd. Bde., which was holding the line.	
	Oct 28th		Was spent in resting and reorganizing. Two hours training was also carried out.	
	Oct 29th		The Battalion moved out at 1300 and marched to t J.31 where it relieved the 11th. Bn. E.Yorks. Regt. in Support. Our Brigade having taken over the line.	

WAR DIARY
or
INTELLIGENCE SUMMARY.
(Erase heading not required.)

Army Form C. 2118.

Place	Date	Hour	Summary of Events and Information	Remarks and references to Appendices
France	1918 Oct 30th		The Battalion remained in this area. Reconnaissance forward was made by Coy. & Platoon Commdrs. & Platoon Sgts. In view of the forthcoming operations, assembly trenches were dug by Coys. in P.4.d.	
	Oct 31st		At 0525 the 94th (Yeo) Inf. Bde. made an attack on the following objectives:- First Objective P.12.d.90.05.-P.12.b.6.3.-P.6.d.1.2.-P.6.Central- J.36.c.8.8. Second Objective Q.8.Central-Q.32.Central The 12th.(Yeo) Bn Norfolk Regt. were in Bde. reserve. The Battalion assembled in the trenches previously dug about 0500. At 0845 when the first objective had been taken, the Battalion moved forward to P.4.d with Bn. H.Q. at P.4.d.9.9. The Battalion remained here in support. Effective Strength:- 42 Officers 800 other ranks.	

WAR DIARY
or
INTELLIGENCE SUMMARY.
(Erase heading not required.)

Army Form C. 2118.

Place	Date	Hour	Summary of Events and Information	Remarks and references to Appendices
France	1918 Oct. 21		The Commdg. Officer received the following message from the 94th (Yeo) Infantry Brigade. Headquarters. 94th.(Yeo) Inf. Bde. "The Corps Commdr. saw the 12th.(Yeo) Bn. Norfolk Regt. on the march today and wishes his congratulations conveyed to the C.O. on the exceptionally good turnout and march discipline of the Battalion with which he was pleased. (Sd.)W.H.Annesley.Lt.Col. 20/10/18. A.A.& Q.M.G. 31st.Div. The following appeared in Army,Corps,Divisional & Brigade Routine Orders. "The following extract from a captured German Regtl. Order shows the excellent behaviour after capture of a patrol from the Norfolk Regt. who were captured by the enemy on the 11th.Sept.1918 near PLOEGSTERRT. The enemy appreciates their soldierly bearing and holds them up to his own men as an example. Method of Capture. "The Prisoners belong to a big patrol ordered to make good the occupation of a farm. (apparently HOF OSTERNELLE near PLOEGSTEERT) and to put out of action the Machine Guns conjectured to be there. The 21 prisoners among whom were 4 N.C.O.s had all taken off their badges and could not or would not give a satisfactory reason for having done so. The great majority of the prisoners belong to the workman class They make a good military impression but in their statements are so extraordinary reticient that one must assume that their superior Officers have instructed them clearly and warned them how to behave when taken prisoners. The G.O.C. feels sure that officers will spare no pains to instruct their men similarly. The G.O.C. congratulates the C.O. & all ranks on the fine spirit shewn by these N.C.O.s & men of the 12th.(Yeo) Bn.Norfolk Regiment. This patrol which was captured, was one found by C Coy. whilst the Battalion was in the line in the PLOEGSTEERT Sector.	

Army Form W.3091.

(6392) Wt. W6192/P875 1,500,000 4/18 McA & W Ltd (E 2815) Forms W3091/4.

Cover for Documents.

Nature of Enclosures.

War Diary
for November, 1918.

12th (Yeo) Bn. R.S.F.

Notes, or Letters written.

WAR DIARY.

OF THE

12th (YEO.) BN NORFOLK Rt

FOR

NOVEMBER
1918

Army Form C. 2118.

WAR DIARY
or
INTELLIGENCE SUMMARY.
(Erase heading not required.)

Instructions regarding War Diaries and Intelligence Summaries are contained in F. S. Regs., Part II. and the Staff Manual respectively. Title pages will be prepared in manuscript.

Place	Date	Hour	Summary of Events and Information	Remarks and references to Appendices
FRANCE	1918 Nov 1-2		The Battalion remained at P.4.d. in support to the two attacking Battns. of the 94th. Brigade.	
	3rd		The Brigade received orders to move back. The Battalion marched to COURTRAI en route to billets at LAUWE.	
	4th		The Battalion moved on to LAUWE, arriving there about 1500 & went into billets.	
	5/6th		The Battalion remained at LAUWE, reorganizing & training.	
	7th		The Battalion received orders to relieve the 7/8 Royal Inniskilling Fus. in the line on the banks of the SCHELDT. with Battalion H.Q. at P.26.b.4.5. The Battalion moved up in lorries(motors), leaving LAUWE at 1300. Relief was completed by w.pp. 2200	
	8th		The Battalion was relieved in the line by the E.Lancs Regt. at 2230 and marched to SWEVEGHEM en route for LAUWE	
	9th		The Battalion left SWEVEGHEM at 0900 and marched through to LAUWE arriving there about 1400 taking over the same billets as previously occupied.	
	10th		The Battalion moved back to AVELGHEM which was part of the area previously held on the 7th. Owing to the long march just completed by the Battalion, motor lorries were provided, and the Battalion arrived at destination about 1430.	
	11th		News was received that the Armistice was signed and a general advance ordered. The Battalion marched to RENAIX going into billets about 1500.	
	12th		The Battalion remained at RENAIX.	
	13th		The Battalion moved back to RUYEN on the SCHELDT, near AVELGHEM, occupying empty houses.	
	14th		The Battalion marched to COURTRAI arriving there at 1500 & occupying billets.	
	15th		The Battalion moved back to LAUWE occupying same billets as before.	
	16th		The Battalion spent this period in reorganizing, refitting. Ceremonial parades both Brigade & Battalion were practised	

WAR DIARY
or
INTELLIGENCE SUMMARY.
(Erase heading not required.)

Army Form C. 2118.

Place	Date	Hour	Summary of Events and Information	Remarks and references to Appendices

FRANCE	22nd 10/4/1		The Brigade paraded for the presentation of medal ribbons to recipients of awards since joining the 51st. Division. The following members of the Battalion received ribbons:-
			     Sgt. Hase D.C.M.
			     L/Sgt. Lawn M.M.
			     Cpl. Lloyd M.M.
			     Cpl. Bunning M.M.
			     Cpl. Gladwin M.M.
			     Pte. Watts M.M.
			     Pte. Blake M.M.
			 The Divisional Commdr. addressed the Brigade complementing them on the services they had rendered during the operations.	

	24th		The Battalion commenced the march to ST. OMER marching out of LAUWE at 0920 arriving at MENIN the first stage at 1200	
	25th		The Battalion moved out of MENIN at 0800 en route for VLAMERTINGHE arriving there about 1600	
	26th		The Battalion left VLAMERTINGHE at 0800 & marched to ST. ELOI area arriving there about 1300	
	27th		The Battalion marched to EBLINGHEM arriving there at 1400 & occupying hutments	
	28th		The Battalion moved out at 0920 and marched to ST MARTIN AU LAERT arriving there at 1300	
	29/31st		This period was spent in cleaning up after the march. One march casualty only was sustained during the whole journey and this man rejoined the Battalion 3 hours after arrival. Effective Strength:- 41 Officers 802 other ranks.	

Commdg. 12th (S) Bn. Norfolk Regt.
Major
W Steward

YB/3

WAR DIARY

OF THE

12TH (YEO.) BN NORFOLK REGT

FOR MONTH OF

DECEMBER 1918.

Army Form C. 2118.

WAR DIARY
or
INTELLIGENCE SUMMARY.
(Erase heading not required.)

Instructions regarding War Diaries and Intelligence Summaries are contained in F. S. Regs., Part II. and the Staff Manual respectively. Title pages will be prepared in manuscript.

Place	Date	Hour	Summary of Events and Information	Remarks and references to Appendices
FRANCE	Dec 1918 1st		Five officers & 8 N.C.O.s. of the Battalion attended a demonstration at the 2nd. Army School VISQUES showing the correct way to drill.	
	4th		The following message was received from Lt.Col.Morse:- Commdg.Officer,12th Yeol.Battalion Norfolk Regiment. "I shall be very grateful if you will convey to all ranks of the Battalion ,at any rate those with whom I served,now sorry I was to leave them in July and to have to say good-bye now. Also how much I appreciate their good work all through the War and their invariable loyalty and good fellowship I look upon them all as personal friends,no man ever had better,and I shall always be delighted to hear from any and to see any of them who come back to NORWICH or any where near to have a chat about old times."	
	6th		The Battalion marched,under the command of the Commdg.Officer to 2nd Army Infantry School WISQUES. to attend a demonstration.	
	15th		The following message from His Majesty the King to 2nd.Army Commander was received:- "I cannot leave FLANDERS without letting you know how sorry I am not to have been able to visit the Second Army and personally to congratulate you on its triumph. During the past few days I have visited with pride and admiration the scenes of the famous Battles with which the name of the Second Army will ever be associated. Rest assured that I follow with keen interest the daily onward march of your columns and I trust that all ranks will soon be comfortably settled in their winter Quarters. GEORGE R.I. "	
	16th 18th 20th		The Battalion marched to VAL DE LUMBRES into new huts. The Regimental "Guidon" arrived from ENGLAND. The Divisional Mounted Sports were held at LONGUENESSE. The Battn. won one event. GENERAL REMARKS. During the month the Battalion did one hours Drill daily(ceremonial) under the Adj. or Asst. Adj. Educational Classes were commenced in accordance with the Army Educational Scheme. Miners & a few long service men were sent home for Demobilization. EFFECTIVE STRENGTH. 41 officers 741 other ranks.	

Thurmore-Kelly Lt.Col.
Commdg.12th.Yeo/.N.Norfolk Regt.

Army Form C. 2118.

WAR DIARY
or
INTELLIGENCE SUMMARY.
(Erase heading not required.)

Vol 14

Place	Date	Hour	Summary of Events and Information	Remarks and references to Appendices
France	1st		**General Remarks:-** The Battalion was employed in drill and General Training during the month Salvage work was also carried out in the WISQUES area. Educational Classes were well attended. 1 Officer and 52 O.R. were demobilized during the month.	
"	2nd		The G.O.C. 94th (Yeo.) Inf. Bde presented French Croix de Guerree's to the following:- Acting R.S.M. Snowling W.E. MM. Sergt. Holman R.P. MM. The Battalion Transport gained the following prizes in the 94th (Yeo.) Inf. Brigade Competition. Best Battalion. 12th (Yeo.) Bn. Norfolk Regt. Best Riding & Pack Animals. 12th (Yeo.) Bn. Norfolk Regt. Best pair of Draught horses. 2nd Prize. The same teams won in the 51st Divisional Competition.	
"	20th		The Battalion moved to CALAIS on Strike Duty.	
"	31st		The Battalion returned early morning to Divisional Area, St.Omer. Effective Strength. 40 Officers. 736 O.R.	

Major.
Commanding 12th (Yeo.) Bn. Norfolk Regt.

WAR DIARY
INTELLIGENCE SUMMARY.

12th Army Form. NORFOLK REGIMENT.

Place	Date	Hour	Summary of Events and Information	Remarks and references to Appendices
	February 1919			
	1-5		This period was spent in General Training. Educational Classes were carried on.	
	6		The Battalion moved to HONDEGHEM for duty at the 2nd Army Stagny Camp.	
	7-28		General Duties were carried out at the 2nd A.S. Camp.	
			General Remarks.	
			4 Officers 280 O.R's were demobilised during the month.	
			Effective Strength 31 - 471	
			Ration Strength 17 - 137	
	28			
			1-3-19.	

H.A. Birkbeck Major
Commanding 12(S) R. Norfolk Regt.

Army Form C. 2118.

12 Norfolk R¹

WAR DIARY
or
INTELLIGENCE SUMMARY.
(Erase heading not required.)

V.8.16

Instructions regarding War Diaries and Intelligence Summaries are contained in F. S. Regs., Part II. and the Staff Manual respectively. Title pages will be prepared in manuscript.

Place	Date	Hour	Summary of Events and Information	Remarks and references to Appendices
	March 1-3		The Battalion was employed on Staging Duties at Hondeghem.	
	4ᵗʰ		The Battalion moved to Moir Camp, St Omer, where a Brigade Camp was formed.	
	5ᵗʰ-31ˢᵗ		Several Duties were carried out in the Camp.	
			General Remarks.	
			7 Officers and 33 O.Rs. were demobilised during the month.	
			Effective Strength 25 – 107.	
			Ration Strength 11 – 54.	
	31ˢᵗ		1-4-19.	

Murray Capt.
for Lieut Colonel.
Commdg. 12/N¹ (Res) Bn. Norfolk Regiment.

1st Norfolk Regt

Vol 17

WAR DIARY
or
INTELLIGENCE SUMMARY.
(Erase heading not required.)

Army Form C. 2118.

Place	Date	Hour	Summary of Events and Information	Remarks and references to Appendices
St Omer France	1st to 30th April 19		The Bn remained at Moir Camp St Omer during the month. During this time the weather has been very unsettled, continually raining. The Bn is now almost reduced to Cadre Strength, and is waiting to move overseas.	
	30/4/19		2 Officers were demobilized during the month. Effective Strength 11 Offrs 45 O.Rs.	

1/5/19.

M A Bryant Capt.
Comndg (10th (Res) Bn Norfolk Regt)

Army Form C. 2118.

12 November 1918

WAR DIARY
or
INTELLIGENCE SUMMARY.
(Erase heading not required.)

Instructions regarding War Diaries and Intelligence Summaries are contained in F. S. Regs., Part II. and the Staff Manual respectively. Title pages will be prepared in manuscript.

Place	Date	Hour	Summary of Events and Information	Remarks and references to Appendices
8th Quse France	1/5/19		This period was spent by the Bn in camp duties and cleaning equipment etc.	Ceases
"	18/5/19		The Bn moved to Wissingensaute for rest remaining until the 19th inst.	
"	19/5/19		Entrained for Dunkirk arrived about 1800 hours.	
	19/5/19 20/5/19		Disembarkation the Bn proceeded to Embarkation Camp to wait for boat.	
	24/5/19		The Bn entrained for U.K. en-b Moyfield.	

D. Mayfield Capt.
Comdg 12th (Res) Bn. Norfolk Regt.